IMAGES OF QUEENSLAND

FRASER ISLAND

Photography

PETER LIK

Tanglewood Press

Front cover: Indian Head
Back cover: Wanggoolba Creek
Title page: Orchid Beach, looking south to
Waddy Point

ISBN 0 947163 44 1

© Tanglewood Press, 1995

Published by Tanglewood Press, an imprint of
GAP Publishing, 44 Wendell St, Norman Park,
Queensland 4170, Australia.

Produced in Hong Kong by Mandarin Offset

Introduction

Fraser Island, situated off the southern Queensland coast, is renowned for its special environmental diversity, and has been protected since 1992 as a World Heritage listing. It is unique as the largest sand island in the world, and is over 120 km in length and covers an area of 165,280 hectares. The visitor is able to enjoy a variety of landscapes, from magnificent stretches of beach to colourful cliffs and gorges, rainforests, freshwater lakes and creeks, and spectacular sandblows. Plant and wildlife species (in particular birds and dingoes) are abundant.

Freshwater creeks, such as Wanggoolba at Central Station, and Eli Creek on the eastern side, are the most prominent of the many creeks on the island.

The water in the lakes on the island is too pure to support much life. An exception is Lake Wabby, which supports several varieties of fish. Lake McKenzie, one of the largest of the lakes, can be viewed from four-wheel drive circuits and walking tracks.

Although Fraser has been heavily logged there are still large stands of satinays, brush-box, piccabeen and kauri palms in the sub-tropical rainforests. In addition to tall forests there are shrublands, scribbly gums and wallum banksia.

The island features sandblows such as Knifeblade, caused by the action of sand shifting across the island. There are seventy-two different coloured sands, the best of which occur north of Happy Valley. Indian head, one of several rocky headlands, is the major landmark of the island, and is found at the northern end of Seventy Five Mile Beach. Further north is Middle Rocks' Champagne Pools, a popular swimming hole. Waddy Point provides fishing and views from the lookout.

Fraser Island is of special importance to Aboriginal people who had inhabited the island for over 5500 years by the time the first Europeans arrived on the mainland. The Butchalla people were the largest group and their lifestyle was relatively tranquil and healthy owing to the abundance of fresh fish, shellfish and fresh water. Middens, formed from discarded shells, are an important archeological record of Aboriginal settlement, and are protected by law.

The major access to the island is by barge and water-taxi, which operate from Hervey Bay. Full and half day tours also operate from Brisbane, the Sunshine coast, Rainbow Beach, Urangan and River Heads. Air charter services are available to the island.

There are a number of places to stay on the island - Eurong Beach Resort, Happy Valley Resort, and Kingfisher Bay Resort and Village. Camping areas are located at Central Station, Lake Boomanjin, Lake Allom, Wathumba, Waddy Point, Lake McKenzie, Dilli Village, Cathedral Beach and Dundubara. Beach camping is also permitted unless signs indicate otherwise. Permits are required for all vehicles, and can be obtained from any of the Department of Environment and Heritage offices.

Fraser Island is the third book in the series entitled 'Images of Queensland'.

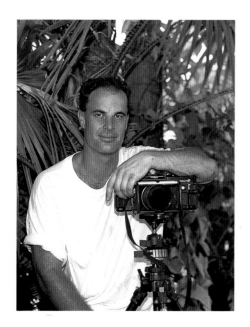

Peter Lik's obsession with photography has taken him on many journeys exploring Queensland and beyond. Using his Fuji 617 panoramic camera, Peter captures the beauty and diversity of Australia's spectacular landscape - from reef to rainforest and from the coast to the outback.

The panoramic technique has become Peter's trademark, and commissions have been forthcoming from companies such as Daikyo, Great Adventures and Queensland Rail. As a contract photographer for the Queensland Tourist and Travel Corporation, Peter's images appear in many publications promoting Queensland worldwide.

Peter Lik's unique photographs of Queensland are to be published in a series of books entitled 'Images of Queensland'.

Indian Head at sunrise

Overleaf: Waddy Point

Lake Garawongera

Wanggoolba Creek

Wanggoolba Creek

Dingo tracks over sand dune at Indian Head

Dingoes are protected on Fraser Island

Knifeblade Sandblow

Sunrise at Yidney Rocks

Sandy Cape

Middle Rocks to Waddy Point

Above and left: Coloured sands, Cathedral Beach

World Heritage Rainforest,Central Station

Overleaf: Sunrise, Cathedral Beach

Canoeing - one of the many recreational
activities available on the island

Kingfisher Bay Resort

Camping near Eurong

Happy Valley Resort

Sand tracks cut through the rainforest

Overleaf: Maheno shipwreck

Indian Head

Overleaf: Waddy Point

Wathumba Creek Estuary

Lake McKenzie

Sunrise at Chard Rocks

Overleaf: Sand dunes, Knifeblade Sandblow

Surf at Middle Rocks

Four-wheel driving between Indian Head
and Waddy Point, near Middle Rocks

Overleaf: Champagne Pools

Indian Head

Sandblows, Cathedral Beach

Main highway near Hidden Lake

Overleaf: Eli Creek

Platypus Bay

Humpback whale off the coast of Fraser Island

Overleaf: Lake McKenzie

Lake Wabby, formed when a sandblow filled a freshwater creek

Overleaf: Sunrise over sandblow near Lake Wabby

Orchid Beach, looking south to Waddy Point

Overleaf: Great Sandy Strait in front of Kingfisher Bay Resort